Parenting with Promises

Debbie Kunz, MSW

Tom
& merryl
Blessings on
this gift!
Hope this
provides helpful
info!
love donathan

May you be encouraged,
renewed and affirmed by the
photos & words of this
book. PEace!
DEbbie
Kunz

WestBow Press books may be ordered through booksellers or by contacting:

WestBow Press
A Division of Thomas Nelson & Zondervan
1663 Liberty Drive
Bloomington, IN 47403
www.westbowpress.com
1 (866) 928-1240

ISBN: 978-1-5127-2953-5 (sc)
ISBN: 978-1-5127-2997-9 (e)

Print information available on the last page.

WestBow Press rev. date: 3/9/2016

WESTBOW
PRESS®
A DIVISION OF THOMAS NELSON
& ZONDERVAN

The Bible is God's written word of His promises to us – His children. *Parenting with Promises* is meant to illustrate these promises in a simple, yet profound way. It is also designed to help parents fill their verbal and non-verbal messages to their children with a Godly unconditional love, while steering their children to the source of all love and forgiveness.

Read this book together with your child, talking about the photographs and the scriptures while discussing God's promises to you. Read the text pages as a parent, soaking in God's promise to you as a person and as a parent, and reflecting on the type of parent you want to be.

Parenting is one of the toughest life journeys and our children will be greatly impacted by the way we express love to them. Allow the scriptures in this book to remind you of God's promises to you so that you might be able to speak those same promises to your most precious gifts – your children.

Love Love

"I have loved you with an everlasting love..."
—Jeremiah 31:3

"[NOTHING] will be able to separate us from the love of God that is in Christ Jesus."
—Romans 8:38

Grace Grace

"For it is by grace you have been saved, through faith...it is the gift of God."

—Ephesians 2:8

"Let us then approach the throne of grace with confidence, so that we may receive mercy and find grace to help us in our time of need."

—Hebrews 4:16

As parents, what does it look like to love our children and offer them grace? **Unconditional love means loving our children no matter what**. Our love is not contingent on their behavior, their choices or their reciprocity. Children who feel secure in their parents' love are free to become the unique people God created them to be. Conveying messages of love to children requires separating a child's behavior from his/her worth. Just as God has called us "worthy" of His love, **our children are WORTHY of our love.** They do not earn our love; rather, we offer it to them as a gift, just as God offers His grace to us as an unearned gift. As they grow secure in our unconditional love, they feel valued, worthy, unique, special, safe and trustworthy.

Coupling grace with love gives us the ability to forgive and empower our children to rebound from their own negative choices or behavior with the confidence that they are still loved and valued.

Reflections on Love and Grace:

1. How was love expressed to you during your childhood?
2. How do you WANT to express love to your child?
3. What is your understanding of God's grace?
4. How do you want your child to experience God's grace? What can you do as a parent to communicate grace to your child?
5. When you feel insecure in God's love, what statements remind you of God's unconditional love for you? How can you put those statements into words for your child?

Parenting with Promises Tip

Unconditional love does not mean "I love you IF" or "I love you BUT." It means "I love you DESPITE"

Peace Peace

"[Jesus] himself is our Peace..."

—Ephesians 2:14

"Now may the Lord of peace himself give you peace at all times and in every way."

—2 Thessalonians 3:16

Safety Safety

"I will lie down and sleep in peace, for you alone, O Lord, make me dwell in safety."

—Psalm 4:8

"So do not fear, for I am with you;
do not be dismayed, for I am your God.
I will strengthen you and help you;
I will uphold you with my righteous right hand."

—Isaiah 41:10

Presence Presence

"Never will I leave you; never will I forsake you."

—Hebrews 13:5

Be strong and courageous. Do not be afraid; do not be discouraged, for the Lord your God will be with you wherever you go."

—Joshua 1:9

Hope Hope

"I wait for the Lord, my soul waits, and in His word I put my hope."

—Psalm 130:5

"Now faith is being sure of what we hope for and certain of what we do not see."

—Hebrews 11:1

Protection Protection

"The Lord watches over you – the Lord is your shade at your right hand…The Lord will keep you from all harm – he will watch over your life; The Lord will watch over your coming and going both now and forevermore."

—Psalm 121: 5-8

"But let all who take refuge in you be glad; let them ever sing for joy. Spread your protection over them, that those who love your name may rejoice in you."

—Psalm 5:11

Life is full of new experiences. Depending on a person's temperament, these new experiences can be met with anticipation and excitement or fear and anxiety. **God promises us that He is always with us and that He can give us His Peace despite our own fear.** Teaching your child to trust this promise will require modeling and verbal reassurance on your part. Children sense our unspoken emotions, and they will learn to be full of fear or peace by observing our reactions to life. When you are feeling fearful or anxious, tell your child that you are scared but that you trust God to be with you. When your child is fearful, pray for God to fill him/her with peace. Although the fear might not immediately subside, you are teaching your child to go straight to the source of all Peace. **As children grow in faith and trust, their fears and anxieties will be replaced by the inexplicable peace that comes from knowing and trusting God.** Their hearts are also full of hope – a hope that is not contingent on the good or bad things happening in their lives, but a hope that trusts in God to be with them in all circumstances.

Reflections of **Peace, Safety, Presence, Hope, and Protection:**

1. What types of situations make you anxious? How do you use your faith to help remind you that God is with you?
2. When life doesn't seem to go the way you want, how do you place hope in God? What words of God give you hope?
3. When you are full of fear, how do God's promises of safety and protection reassure you? Are you open to God's safety and protection not looking like you thought it would?

Parenting with Promises Tip:

Allow your children to experience their emotions, giving them an "emotional vocabulary" (telling them what they are feeling) and teaching them how to respond to the emotion.

Strength Strength

"The joy of the Lord is my strength."

—Nehemiah 8:10

"I can do everything through [Christ] who gives me strength."

—Phillipians 4:13

Purpose Purpose

"For we are God's workmanship, created in Christ Jesus to do good works, which God prepared in advance for us to do."

—Ephesians 2:10

Life Life

"God, who is rich in mercy, made us alive in Christ."

—Ephesians 2:4-5

"When Jesus spoke again to the people, he said, 'I am the light of the world. Whoever follows me will never walk in darkness, but will have the light of life.'"

—John 8:12

Provision Provision

"I am the bread of life. He who comes to me will never go hungry, and he who believes in me will never be thirsty."

—John 6:35

"Therefore, I tell you, do not worry about your life, what you will eat or drink; or about your body, what you will wear… Look at the birds of the air; they do not sow or reap or store away in barns, and yet your heavenly Father feeds them. Are you not much more valuable than they?"

—Matthew 6:25-26

What are the unique characteristics of your child? Is she curious, high-spirited, analytical, intense, happy, easygoing? Is he similar to you in personality or different than you? **Sometimes we want our children to be something specific, often overlooking who they are created to be.** From an early age, children show us what their unique attributes are. Pay attention to your child's interests and abilities; ask for his input regarding daily activities; honor his requests and capitalize on his strengths. As you teach your child about her unique contributions to the world, point out your similarities and differences. **Help your child see value in others, not assuming that she needs to be like others or that others need to be like she is.** God has blessed us each differently so that together we might make up a collective body of Christ. We are interdependent; we need each other. Helping our children figure out who they are contributes to the health of the entire body of Christ.

Your children are "yours," but are they YOU? They are "yours" in the sense that you are a steward to the gift God has given you. Ultimately, we are all God's children, and God is the one who has created us to make our unique mark on this world. **In His divine wisdom, God created us all differently so that we might have completeness in the community He creates.** No person can make it alone. When children have parents who embrace their uniqueness, they grow in confidence and purpose, striving for the life that God has created them to live.

*the pronoun "his" or "her" is used interchangeably.

Reflections on *Strength, Purpose, Life and Provision:*

1. What purpose do you think God has for you? How can you convey confidence to your child that he/she has purpose?
2. When you are tempted to rely on yourself for you own provision, how do you remind yourself that God is the giver of all life, and that God will supply your needs?
3. What does your child seem to enjoy doing? How do her interests teach you about what unique talents she has?
4. What does the Bible teach us about strength? Who is the source of all strength? When we rely on God's strength, what emotion do we experience?

Parenting with Promises Tip:

Choose one activity to do every day that communicates love to your child. It might be snuggling together, playing together, reading a book together or wrestling. It does not matter WHAT the activity is; what matters is that your child feels special and worthy of your time, and ultimately loved by you.

Forgiveness Forgiveness

"Be kind and compassionate to one another, forgiving each other, just as in Christ God forgave you."

—Ephesians 4:32

"I, even I, am he who blots out your transgressions, for my own sake, and remembers your sins no more."

—Isaiah 43:25

"As far as the east is from the west, so far has he removed our transgressions from us."

—Psalm 103:12

Compassion Compassion

"The Lord is gracious and compassionate, slow to anger and rich in love."

—Psalm 145:8

"Therefore, as God's chosen people, holy and dearly loved, clothe yourselves with compassion, kindness, humility, gentleness and patience."

—Colossians 3:12

Joy Joy

"Clap your hands, all you nations; shout to God with cries of joy."

—Psalm 47:1

"Though you have not seen Him, you love Him; and even though you do not see Him now, you believe in Him and are filled with an inexpressible and glorious joy."

—1 Peter 1:8-9

Of all of God's promises to us, forgiveness is the most powerful, and oftentimes the most difficult to accept. **Throughout the Bible, we learn about God's expression of forgiveness through His mercy and compassion.** When Jonah was hard-hearted, God sent him shade. When the Israelites complained about God's provision in the daily showering of manna, God gave them meat. When the prodigal son returns home repentant, his Father welcomes him with open arms and throws a party for him.

Through His word, God demonstrates His love and forgiveness to us despite our own stubbornness, selfishness, and ingratitude. In fact, God loves us so much that He sacrificed His son for our sins. **Jesus washed our sins white as snow; Jesus offered us promises of a future. Jesus gave us life!**

As a parent, trust God's promise of forgiveness and demonstrate that same forgiveness to your children. When your children defy you, disrespect you, and disobey you, show them compassion and open your arms to them. **Forgiving your children does not mean approving of their behavior; forgiving means relentlessly loving despite the behavior.** It also means allowing the emotions of the moment to wash away in the flood of forgiveness. You will not dwell on the child's mistakes; instead, you will empower the child by allowing each moment and each day to be refreshingly new.

Accepting forgiveness allows us to move forward in joy, confident that God loves us.

Reflections on *Forgiveness, Compassion and Joy*

1. When you make poor choices, how are you able to seek and experience God's forgiveness? When you allow God to forgive you, do you sense His compassion? Are you renewed with a joy that comes from a Father who never withholds love from you? How does that joy give you strength?

2. What does compassion mean to you? Can a parent show compassion and yet also be firm?

3. Think about a time a person betrayed you and you had trouble forgiving that person. What was the outcome? Were you able to ultimately forgive? How did you feel after you forgave that person? Now recall a time you did something that required forgiveness. Were you offered forgiveness from the other person? If not, were you able to accept God's forgiveness? How does embracing forgiveness help you move forward?

Parenting with Promises Tip:

Do not assume that your children know how they are supposed to behave. Make sure you tell the child what you expect. Phrase the expectations in a positive way, expressing what you want to see rather that what you don't want to see. "Keep your hands to yourself" is a teaching expression. "Don't hit your brother" is an admonition and can lead to a power struggle.

Eternal Life

"Now we see but a poor reflection as in a mirror; then we shall see face to face. Now I know in part; then I shall know fully, even as I am fully known."

—1 Corinthians 13:12

Final Thoughts and Reflections

God's word is full of promises to us – promises of the purpose we have in this world because of His promise of LOVE to us. He tells us that He knows us inside and out, that He doesn't make mistakes and that His creation is good.

That means that you are good. That means that your children are good.

Does that mean that our behavior is "good" all the time? No, it means that what God created is good and that He created us to live in relationship with Him and fulfill His purpose for us. It means that God loves us despite our good or bad choices. As a source of encouragement and empowerment to us, God sent His Holy Spirit who dwells in us and allows us to produce the fruit of God's goodness – "fruit" such as love, joy, peace, patience, kindness, goodness, faithfulness, gentleness and self-control.

As a parent, you will have the largest single human influence on your child. Cherish this precious gift and lead your child to trust in God by allowing the Holy Spirit to fill your heart with God's promises to you.

Through God's promises to us, we experience the freedom that comes from acceptance of our inheritance as children of a living God. This book highlighted some of God's promises to us:

LOVE   GRACE   PEACE
SAFETY   PRESENCE   HOPE
PROTECTION   STRENGTH   PURPOSE
LIFE   PROVISION   FORGIVENESS
COMPASSION   JOY   ETERNAL LIFE

Use these Biblical promises to increase your trust in God. Believe the words of love to you, and use the scriptures to change any negative self-talk to words of truth. When you tell yourself "I SHOULD have" or "I NEED to" or "If I _____, then God will love me," you are negating God's gift of grace. Instead, **embrace the truth that Christ died for your sins and your God is full of mercy, compassion and love.** You do not need to fear vengeance or retribution. Your heart can be full of **Hope, Joy and Peace!**

Reflections on God's Promises:

1. Which promise is the hardest/easiest for you to believe?
2. What will help you trust God's words of Love for you?
3. How can you share God's promises with your children and with others?

Label each picture with one of God's Promises.

Special thanks to all of the parents and children who allowed us to photograph them for the book

About the photographer:

Sarah Zahnd is an accomplished portrait photographer. She works alongside her husband who together own and operate award winning Zahnd Photography. Sarah is passionate with a keen eye to capture the best of children in photos. Her favorite subjects are her two daughters.

She is also a published writer. Her work has been featured in national and local magazines. You can find more of her work at zahndphotography.com

About the author:

Debbie has been a parent educator for twenty years and is passionate about helping parents be the best parents they can be. She understands the developmental and social-emotional value of parents reading with their children and wants parents to use this book to teach their children and to reflect on their own parenting.

http://www.facebook.com/ParentingWithPromises
Twitter - @ParentWPromise
parentingwithpromises@gmail.com

CPSIA information can be obtained
at www.ICGtesting.com
Printed in the USA
LVOW05s2016140316

479144LV00003B/4/P